Satie's Sad Piano

Satie's Sad Piano

a long poem by

Carolyn Marie Souaid

For Maurice ~ With thanks for "letting me be first." All best, Carolyn M. We ain't broke yet café October 24, 2005.

George Amabile, Editor

Signature

EDITIONS

Cover design by Doowah Design.
Photo of Carolyn Marie Souaid by Danny Harwood-Farkas.

Acknowledgements
A work of the imagination, this book takes liberties with details from the lives of Canada's former "First Family." References to Pierre Elliott Trudeau, his sons, and former wife have been sourced from the news media and filtered through a creative lens, and are in no way intended to constitute the Truth.

Thanks to:
The *Conseil des arts et des lettres du Québec* for the financial support that enabled me to "birth" this book; the Abbaye Cistercienne d'Oka for feeding the imagination; Denise Roig for initiating me to our writing retreats; and George Amabile, my editor, for his unwavering enthusiasm and good critical advice. Finally, thanks to Endre Farkas for friendship and for being an invaluable creative sounding board.

I am also grateful to Michel and Alex, as always, for enduring the process, and to the editors of *Matrix* and *Vallum* magazines who first accepted some of these poems, or versions of them, for publication.

We acknowledge the support of The Canada Council for the Arts and the Manitoba Arts Council for our publishing program.

Printed and bound in Canada by AGMV Marquis.

Library and Archives Canada Cataloguing in Publication

Souaid, Carolyn Marie, 1959-
    Satie's sad piano / Carolyn Marie Souaid.

Poems.
ISBN 1-897109-01-6

    1. Québec (Province)—Social life and customs—20th century—Poetry.

2. Montréal (Québec)—Social life and customs—20th century—Poetry.
I. Title.

PS8587.O87S28 2005   C811'.54   C2005-901252-8

Signature Editions P.O. Box 206, RPO Corydon, Winnipeg, Manitoba, R3M 3S7

Contents

Characters / Voices

Venus

Poet, her teacher & lover

Rose, a fetus

Pierre Elliott Trudeau, in absentia

Mont Royal, a mountain with a view

Radio, medium & "commentator"

The Apostle

Letters

Es tan corto el amor, y es tan largo el olvido.
— Pablo Neruda

Love is so short, and forgetting is so long.

Prologue

The New Millennium

The bishops feared a dip on Wall Street,
flash floods, tornadoes, snow squalling
in tongues, the chickens awry,

      — a white, interstellar madness.

They predicted the harvest in tatters,
provisions under the staircase
stupefied into dust.

The prescient would hear it coming:
a week early, demons in the glassware,
heirloom dinner plates shifting
imperceptibly,

a chink in the rattling air.

They feared 40 days & 40 nights
of blighted, non-believers
spitting up blood, bile, the Seven Deadly Sins
of the rainbow

bruised & shaken, the last conscious radio
issuing prayers for the End.

But midnight came & went, dragging its long face,

& spring arrived, as always: seeded
with light.

Part One

(2000)

September 28, 2000 — Canadians tuned into radio get the official word sometime after 3 pm — former Prime Minister Pierre Elliott Trudeau is dead. And while the country busies itself coping with the aftershock, the news sends Venus, a 50-something woman, suddenly, unexpectedly, into a downward spiral through memories of a past love affair.

Radio

1

Snoozing, she's the tinsel village
in a snowglobe.

Living on borrowed time.
Protective blue shell
of sky overhead.

Rest assured, I will scramble it up.
Buzz the brittle orb
of her skull, discombobulating

the brain. Her sane galaxy
of neurons, short-circuited —

Santa in a flap, shimmying
red up the chimney.

Poinsettias aghast. The children, too,
in hats and scarves, skating

clear off the grid, pond cracked,
their shrink-wrapped screams
scaring light into figure eights.

A whole new blizzard
shaking down.

2

weather forecast   grey today with winds gusting to 35 kilometres per hour   we interrupt this program to bring you   the rain   this rush transcript   *they called it Trudeaumania*   downtown cloudy with patches of overnight fog   minus one degree celsius   if a new roof is in your plans, we can help   *just watch me*   topping the hour daddy, why can't you breathe?   daddy, are you going to die?   for more, visit www.stoptobacco.ca   this late-breaking news   but first, sports   how many people renting an apartment these days don't have insurance?   pick up the phone and find out how little it costs   940 News and CNN covering Montreal and the world   bringing you the business travellers' forecast   wind picking up with a high today of eleven   hot off the wire   Nortel boosts TSE while the dollar slumps experience the finest Italian dishes in the city   downtown arteries all working well   mixed skies tomorrow   more at the bottom of the hour   again, that confirmed   we interrupt our regular program this just in   traffic up next   we interrupt this program

FORMER PRIME MINISTER PIERRE ELLIOTT TRUDEAU DEAD AT 80

3

HEADLINE — *Legendary Icon Paddles*
Downstream. No shirt, no tie,
no flashy red convertible.

No moxie heroics.
Just some Indian fringe
and his grave bequest:

Balance. Even strokes
in the red canoe.

Reason separates us

from the apes. Truth.
The wrong pair of shoes
can spark a diplomatic fuss.

Live in a fishbowl

with your Chippendale chairs,
your clean white socks,

and God.

Honour the frisson in your heart,
the backhand pirouette,

baring itself to you.

4

Wind-flung butterfly, she spun.
Like Dorothy vortexing

backwards through the Kansas Bowl.
Sucking in gravity by the dustful.

Rough-shooting the atmosphere,
re-entering it on a wing

and a prayer. Another go

at her china-blue days on earth,
pupa wedged in her plush château.

Kleenex, coins, regrets

fathomed deep
in her pockets.

Secrets, I meant.

Fixing to break free.

Mont Royal

1

Here, straight-up, folks, the facts minus the static, the splutter, the
weather, minus the rupture, the rapture, the shock, the shaggy-dog
hyperbole, the catscruff, the crossed wires, parentheses

Here is V driving conspicuously fast,
her windshield smudged, the hood sweating leaves

Here, too, is the evening sky tuned in, aghast —
Aphrodite, swerving recklessly among the planets

Here is the hurtling, scorching, meowling
past that burns, regrets:
an amorous Romeo groping the balcony

And here, swamped by the hordes, is the other one, the darling,
right and honourable, a rose in his lapel

Here is the Plague on the House,
the Machiavellian machinations.

Here is Shakespeare at the inkwell,
orchestrating tragedy

Here, distilled, after four hundred years,

minus the rhetoric, is Act Four, scene one, spilled
upon the parchment —

Venus smiles not in a house of tears

2

Call it an average day, people puttering off in cars,
waving their simple goodbyes,

weekday wired with comings and goings.
The focus always forward, upbeat:

the exuberant arrival, a destiny
lush and green,

the plucky air blown in from Belize.

Routine, yes, though dawn is sluggish
and unpredictable, a certain melancholy

clouding the sky. An exception to the rule,
forecast one Biblical, metaphoric night:

Three Wise Men, one stooped alone.

His jeweled question wrapped in simple cloth
for the stars. To stay or to go?

And then an unexpected turn of events.

No deep magisterial voice booming down
from above, but serenity inserting itself,

resignation. The whitest angel hair
snowing down on him, hushed.

3

Reports of his death
were greatly exaggerated —

Spode, Bakarra, Red-Eye, St-Tropez

a fine bone plate of chèvre

crudités

crystal cut with Chardonnay

the bereft
ex-wife sipping what's left

of romance

in the estranged
three o'clock light

summer shifting off,
taking flight

for eternal France

4

What he left behind
when the story broke:

the mythology of an era.

A generation lost
in the garden.

Eden writhing
in our collective imagination.

Fine-spun silk
in the rough of town.

He left what was cut
from darkness,

what was nestled,
with love,
in the crook of the road.

A boy, a girl
and the raw piece of flint
that kept them warm.

5

Tonight, the posthumous world in full swing,
news items packing their low, quick punches to the heart:
the debauched, the diabolical, the Twin explosions
already hatching in another hemisphere, beacons
for geese on their empty flight home.

The bump and grind of an ordinary day. Blink once,
and you'd miss it, like you might miss this town,
drained, starved for action.

Alert, you'd see a metered pulse stuttering,
fighting to make a comeback,
the faint static and crackle,

a radio frequency nose-diving.

You'd see how some go looking for loss, for drama,
their entire body cherried into range,
vulnerable, like the open prairie
in the eye of the storm,

waiting for it to happen, knowing it will, crescendo,
the sky caving in,

the unavoidable holocaust
of light.

6

Even in death, he looms
larger than life,

dovetailing

with the sodium clouds
& the gun-slung cold.

Rinsing back down over the city.

She trudges. Vectors, they all trudge
home to their davenports
& dour TVs.

Would she could wield
her ponderous thoughts,

pull souvenir swatches
from the aquarelle sky.

7

What does it mean to say

someone shook in the last moments of his skinny life?

Emphasis on the word *skinny*.

I'm thinking the inconsequential Portuguese guy
wheeling his home around on a shopping cart.
Head flapjacked with a dozen toques.

Or the subordinate checkout clerk at K-Mart,
not just out of chemo, not even a single mom
busting her ass to put a bone on the table,
just working the drudge because she's too damn lazy
to lug her melons to the welfare line.

Not the really really miniscule, vile but unforgettable:

Lee Harvey Oswald. Sirhan Sirhan.

I mean the lowly nickel-and-dimers,
trifles, slugs that flicker twice, thrice,
before permanently scrolling up into themselves
and worming underground.

The half-hearted rot in my vegetable patch,
barely fragrant, barely visible,
that struggles out of nowhere.

Inching, like a common star, through mud.

Making its small, sad go of it.

8

In his basement flat, a man puts the final touches
to a letter. Editing words, two or three at a time,
until his erratic pulse flattens
into greytone across the page.

The trick is to avoid emotion, erase doubt

especially now, at this critical juncture.
When strolling couples flock the censored light,
drawing momentum

from the vigorous spurt of fall —
scarlet ruckus of leaves, fighting
to hang on. Taking their cue

from even the slightest things: field mice.
Their excitable whispers scuttling the wind.

Upstairs, a rose is dying.

Or trying to. Still too stubborn,
too flushed with time
to let a gentle tug,
magnetic earth, pull it under.

Venus

1

There was never any summer to begin with.
Or maybe, maybe it just abandoned us
weeks before the chirping light could stir
the tight-lipped greens of spring.

What do I know?

This quiet patch of weeds leaning in
from the graveyard, leaving

a small depression in the air.

Turned down work today, couldn't stand
the thought of all those hungry faces
looking to me for answers.

2

By whose leaden will did I fall
into fall's most alluring musk?

Who deranged the senses

such that I nosed beyond the knowable
road, the tactile

alligator bark of trees?

Who sent me gibbering into my
simple, primitive brain?

Father, I know not that I have sinned,
merely this:

I would as soon travel blind
as inhabit earth's pedestrian corridors.

Lured by the cinnabar waltz
of leaf on leaf,
gold sniffing out rust.
Delusional.

Love thrown, whimsically,
my way.

3

everything points to your
absence:

dimmed tail lights of cars & outgoing geese
the grim, subtracted leaves

a bristled, Andean chill to the air

you on exotic soil
     — I, exiled

in the long, wan shade
of home

metaphors not of sadness, really

but of the enormity
of unneeding you

this late in the afternoon

4

Sliver of a man, Father lived buried
under detail. Whole white nights clutching

duct tape and a dog-eared list, stretching to save
a buck here, buck there. Realized the value

of things, the whys of keeping a snack
on hand for emergencies.

Made his usual rounds before bed,
padlocking every door, every crack.

The real fear not the thief inside, but the house
suddenly, irrationally, bloating with light.

I dismissed him, as kids do, downplayed
his perpetual heartburn,
his mouse-at-the-kichen-table stance.
Panic afloat in a glass of seltzer water.

Because Montreal was spritzing
into a glitzy Ferris wheel,

because front lawns were growing up
taller than the fences containing them,

because the fabled yellow brick road
paved with sin and debauchery

was belting for me at a crazed clip,
carrying a world I couldn't accommodate
fast enough.

        The enigmatic wind swept me away.

Most terrified, my dad hung back.

Clinging to his honest crumb of land. So the rest
of us, the bloodline, could *live*.

5

I only nodded off a moment.

Dreaming the train again, luggage
embarking & disembarking, synchronized
to the tiered anatomy
of the land: the trenchant peaks, glaciers
hemorrhaging into the great cities —
a streamlined paradise of men.

I saw the pearl of injustice, germinating:
toughbacks cleaving the virtuous soil,
the gash aggrandizing
under their picks.

I witnessed the cooling of time,
the congealed scar
stretching west to east,
names sewn seamlessly into history.

But, there were footnotes to the field notes.

Women, no less, manning sweat from their brow,
their ladylike ruffles rough with toil.

When I woke, a century
had passed.

Rose

1

Did the shroud of dawn
awaken you?

Or was it the cunning
wind of Hades, come to you

in sleep, whispering dreams
of earth

trodden & worn to ash?

A word
alone
can veil all hope

&

death is just another day
we open to.

2

Don't be surprised. I'm still here,
webbing the dark with every other abomination:
the two-headed, the rancid,
the upside-down. Fuzzy approximations
spidering God's spare rooms.

What we lack in heft, we provide in wit.

I'm the aborted air, atomized.
The sea's frail spume.

I'm the insufficient light at your back.
Here, not in breath, but in the speechless murk
in the marsh of your tongue. Dwarfed, fallow

because I couldn't assimilate, couldn't swallow
the stretch marks on the planet.
The compromised sun.
Dogs, all of you, salivating to a bell.

Your curt, manufactured smiles for the photographer.

Like them, I pictured a different hell:
The wholesome world, warmth, a bed.

Days before my birth hour, I stood outside
your apartment walls, weeping.

3

Beyond the instant, there is history,
loss, rooted in the gene pool of a city,
rusted into its ancestry.

You smell it in the air.

The elusive Northwest Passage, a scarcity
of tea. Greenish, stegosaural hulks nailed
over the river: the Navigators.
Jacques Cartier, Champlain.

Les filles who set sail, uncanonized.
Oxidizing on infant soil.

This is what lushes life,
fleshes it out.

Each moment, part of a greater genealogy.
Branch after branch twigging backwards
to the ghost nugget.

Gentrify the industrial park, but in its heart
of hearts, a condo is still an abbatoir.

Take a moment like this.
You are alone, driving recklessly.
The radio is on, and you are all ears.
There is talk:

Trudeau has died.

Your sadness, shock shatters the singularity.

Suddenly, unexpectedly, we are two
careening down the highway.

You and I in the same humidity,
at opposite ends of living.
Your solid mind yielding

to the shards: a weak, past-tense
rose minnowing in the morgue.

The crashed histories piling up.

You lurch to a stop, your heart impounded,
the car coughing its way to the side of the road.

You wonder what might have been,
given another moment,
a different set of circumstances.

A softer, leafier stretch.

Hands clasped, communing,
we might have hunkered down
with a cup of chai and a cinnamon bun,

and watched the house where he lay dying,

the interred, half-mast sun
underground.

4

Grieving, you disregard the template.

Drifting with chamomile & caftan & the involuntary
kick of blood, no distraction large enough,
disarming enough

not even the city holing-in, grey, crass,
through a frail screen, the feral fumes.

And if I muddled your here-and-now, what then?

Breached the amniotic wasteland & touched you,
tweaking the blur into shapes you would know:
hemlines on the rise, the city walls, shaking.

I would start here, stoking the fire.
Ebullient rue Sainte-Famille.

Lovers spiralling up the broken stairs,
his lilting breath on your bare birthright.

I would ready you, steady you for *The Flood*,
for lascivious, blackwater rum

& the last, momentous quiver
of love. I would conjure
a rose for the Dead One,

float Eliot, elegiac, in lieu of the moon.

5

Look past your sloped shoulder to the mountain
on the wall: evidence I exist, hardcore proof
of companionship. Symbiotic love.

Travel your eye up the grainy, moth-eaten spine
to the summit. Understand this as the geography

of your own making. The one black mark on your life.

Add a fortress to the scene, a humpback medieval castle.
Sit Mozart at the organ, pounding the maniacal keys.

Now you're ready. Consider the event

incidental. Nine, almost ten, months after the Scare.
Gloom corroding the soupy air:
pigeons, headstones,

a light, industrial rain.

The sun limped out at 6:49. At three, the wind took a ride
in its smudged, grey hearse.

Ignore the room, ignore the lighting, which is all wrong,
ignore the table and its meandering wood grain,
the chipped vase, ignore the rose,
which never really bloomed before going black.

Trust the emotion, instead, the fisted pain,
the abstraction,

the godawful, stratified darkness
heaped, in perpetuity, on your back.

6

You finally capitulate: the sadness, the empty house, the cat
neglecting you for gainful *amour*:

your radiator, a television. Even my phantom cloud of electrons
hovering beyond reach. Nearly human.

Now remember the others.
Those who, like interim spring, lived.

Micha — young, bright, the enamoured sun rising
and setting in his eyes. While I, myself, aged in the cellar

like a bad wine. Vinegar scowling through the acrimonious
dust. Seeing him that day in Kokanee, small and helpless

in glaciered November. A feeble grip on life,
but grip, nonetheless. Such envy in my bones,

such welled-up ice as I watched from the sidelines —
his last hurrah with the avalanching light.

Sky, rock, every reflected detail radiant in the lake.
The one snag, those asparagus-tipped greens spearing

straight for hell. His fate sealed: a body, like mine,
in absentia, and twisted beyond blue.

Pierre, Margaret, the brothers, silhouetted in grief.
Do you know that I nearly laughed out loud?

Till seeing that copious light at his wake: candles, lanterns,
hurricane lamps. Flash photography. Tributes from far and wide

haloing down, forming a human sun around them.

Mont Royal

1

How we become what we become in this life,
I wonder. How many grey newsreel images
are cushioned in the archival cortex?

Waiting to be categorized.

Who knows, beyond doubt, what enticed him,
what lured him to look beyond the immediate:

hallways forking into hallways, a meander
through Mesopotamia, whatever sprang to mind
when he opened Plato or Aristotle.

Perhaps the things he saw as a boy
staring onto Durocher: the universe
between the seeded grass
and the infinite sky.

Look hard enough, you'll find it.

The silver pulse through a restless pond.

A robin winking from the foxglove
after its elated flight through space.

Of course, there's the other theory, too.

That he'd always gone against the grain,
a born wayfarer forever negotiating
the impossible road

between colour-plated reality
and the fantastic.

2

We desired a god, bedrock, the model
Spartan, mind and muscle
armed for calamity,

insurrection. Which arrived ubiquitously
in the guise of poetry: metred clash
of line and space. Carnage
in virgin country.

Election eve, 1968, televised.
Silence bludgeoned with crowbars
and bats and the Latinate yelp of blood:

Death to the hypocrite!
Maudit traître!

This is how he came to us: cool, detached.
With unblinking panache.

Heavens cocktailed with Molotov.

This, especially, about him:
his carnivorous, adversarial dance.
Centre stage, despite the hissing
soda just missing him
by the bare length of a javelin.

Who knew how to win, but mostly
how to fight the fight. A man of letters, too.
Homer with a mean streak.

Shrugging off victory, applause,
with shy but stately precision.
British until the bitter end.

Evening, in ruins, at his feet.
Strewn with the gurglings of loss,
his shattered opponents, down.

3

Assume that nothing has happened.
Consider the impossibility of motion.

Assume that for V to have plummeted,
there must first have been a trajectory:
a warrior, like Mars, brazen enough to take her
by surprise.

His one gift a beguiling apology for lust.
A rose to make amends.

Zeno said: *distance can never be travelled.*
That to get halfway somewhere,
you must go halfway, first.
And so on.

Infinitely hairsplitting the space between points.
It is a paradox. It is civilization

leaping backward into the past,
mammoth footsteps carrying us here
to the eve of melancholy.
Before the rose & its powdery
last breath on earth.

Watch the actors meet: in the carnage of winter.
Magnetic moon galvanizing their extremities.
He tomming after her. She, in a flurry,
mouse-holing for the dark.

What, then, when she emerges from a snowdrift, skittish?

Their territorial games consummated.

Or not. Paradoxically, here, the scene would vaporize, elusive.
Hopscotch us back to her schoolgirl past, halving her life
again & again, in its eternal regression of mirrors.

Ultimately returning her to the start:
she, a grain of sand, coddled
on the virgin shore.

All hint of the end bleached & rinsed away.

Take a look at her, inert, embryonic,
gazing up at the cloud where God lies
cooing on his back: an infant

himself, reduced
to his own babbling light.

Assume that nothing has happened.
Consider Zeno

&

the impossibility of motion.

Picture love still
Septembering
in the speedway

of your heart.

4

After months avoiding the place, she returned
to intractable austerity.

Quebec and the Pope.

Granite gods on twin pedestals
blessing the masses: smallfolk

shoeing through hectares of snow
for sickly branches of their family tree.

Yes-men in the dark, must-filled lounges
of town, spreading disease,

more of the bronze and cavernous world.

Until sentiment exploded, time bombs
assembling in piety,
the detonated heartbeats of men

underground. That year, she voted

for the treasonous light.
Spent tangy June floating
pandemonium

her spry, fresh-air leap spreading beyond
the quarantine

toppling the riot police, Duplessis.

Look, you still see traces —
cathedrals lifting out of the grizzled realm,

skylight parachuting in.

5

Now study her as a girl in the upshot of spring.
Half-grown but leggy, still.

Sins barely filling a postcard — marginalia
anchored off the turquoise coast,
schooner-white, a squiggle of fish.

Naughty, yes, but subtly so.

Lushing herself behind the magnolia
or bunched in among the lilacs,
her filly slit weeping
warm champagne.

Later, on the front lines,
chronicled, the aphrodisiacs —
Hendrix, firebombs, Vietnam.

That bold, swashbuckling Hero in town
accumulating the ladies, sweeping them
upward into euphoria, the clouds, into
wiggy voluptuousness.

But back to her in sheepish recline,
play-acting

the voluminous, rubenesque toss
of mane and hip.

6

Here, in a photograph, she resembles Ophelia
before the ragged blooms washed her downstream

full nectarine moon in her eyes.

Freeze-framed, the purest description
of what it means to be

star-swept & pregnant
with the crumbs of love:

building a nest, making him happy.

From outer space after four centuries,
the same orbiting world.

The woman, barefoot, mothering
his wash in a pail,

her heart, a small doting quadrant
on the wall, bluish, but also
an offering, open season —

her Hamlet all wrapped up in his own
dashed planet.

7

The other image, unshot,
is the one in her mind, digital

diorama of arctic precision.
Where, limned by the sun,

celestial, she's a ray too bright
for the human eye, white

tulle gown filling the frame
with largesse.

Her happiness multiplied
substantially.

Infectious.

As when baby's breath,
startled from the bush,

confettis

into asterisks &
exclamation marks.

Excessive thrill
of snow in the air.

8

Later, in the bath —

She soaps in nostalgia.
Another time, another place.
World redrawn with an artist's hand.

Not the clinical sky, but ocean's
whale-blue back. Foghorn
blowing diaphanous O's.

Eventually, people.
The altered light.

Two figures, no —
one

on the dwindled sand, rock
she'd once dreamt

invincible.

Part Two

(1968)

Montreal, through a kaleidoscope.
Season of candied perception. Incendiary Knowledge.
Sandalwood. Blake from the stars —

He who does not imagine a stronger and better light
Than his perishing and mortal eye can see,
Does not imagine at all.

Mont Royal

1

You ask with trepidation —
how time wizens to this.
Rigor mortis. Life's crushed years in a box.
A rose, face down in the dust,
shrunken, black.

Knowing his fate, Icarus
in the labyrinth, longing to fly,
you wonder —
would he have borne the showy wings,
the rush & ride of beginnings,

would he have chanced the sky?
Would he have bested Kerouac, nerving
for madness on a cock-fool whim,
the sun's mescaline kiss
at his back?

— *Yes.*

2

Yes, she said, her winged heart pumping
beyond the metronome

&

the measured, onward beat of modernity.
Loathing the riff of temperate company girls.

Yes to Marrakesh & mangoes, she said.

Yes to the madrigal sky & to life
          pointing like a gun at her head,

opening fire, fortissimo.

The Apostle

1

Crazed with the scent of my loved-on thumb
is it any wonder I am still here,
rocking the air, a moving soliloquy
of breast & hip? This is why I have come:
to show you things. Winter unmasked, the astonished
enjambment of honey & light. My monkey gods
loosing the wind into trees,
conjuring fruit.

Listen: There's no trick to being content in the world.

It's the other life, the one given to lunacy,
to the endlessly subdividing cells — that's the challenge.
The inert flesh lifting.

Lilacs in profusion. Their unrepressed seepage.

What some, in this dark age,
would call *joy*.

2

Study the seething bulb seconds before twitching out.
Lightningsnap when the human eye still

fathoms objects in a room, skeletons
freeze-framed by the waning filament,

the sick one burning up with fever,
fighting for a last orange breath.

When, afterwards, you study this death
in your hands

when gently, reverently, you shake the bulb
from side to side, listening

for the planetary disturbance, evidence of life lived
and lost, when carefully you consider

the glassed-in whispers of those rasping
two or three grains of sand

the truth suddenly dawns. Words, burning the hand,
lift us through life: *lust, jealousy, desperation.*

Propel us with their gravity, immensity.

Utterances, fragments, bewitching tungsten screams
that momentarily unground us, yank the struggling wick

of our flesh up, up beyond where autumn lies
content in the muslin grass.

Somewhere light-years beyond the sane
blue curvature of Earth, beyond galactic dust.

3

To abandon yourself, absolutely.
To lie among crowds
and not even recognize you are in the city.
A crucifix somewhere in the sky, stars,
the scrambled airwaves.

To lie there, in the evening grass,
hazy, spread-eagled, his galactic weight
miraculously weightless.

To reject ordinary and sufficient language: *soft, gentle.*
Words paler than the torn white blooms of June.

To let the god of Hades pluck you like the last furred peach
from a tree — to not even know this

— and then sink, dreamily, willingly down into where
the hyacinth landscape withers and withdraws.

To beat the same blood, wing for wing,
as the blue-black raven. To forget
your goodbyes, grace, the memory of the tongue
inside the mouth, breath.

To let the feathered rain salvage you, even when there is no rain.

To be innocent, vile, wayward, translucent,
all these colours — at once.

To be darkness, a stranger, in your own body.

4

this gene
governing
obsession

barely the
wingtip

of a spark

or Cupid's
flung dart

less than zero :

: so small a squint
won't summon it

say, negative space
on the Y-axis

where a thin dime
dropped sideways
into snow shivers
invisibly

materializing

paler than the
palest January light
next spring

hand's heart's
astonishing find

5

And if geography annotated the particulars?
Every living, breathing detail of the highway.
A trip, say, to the coast of Maine.

What landmarks between there and love?

Vistas of sienna beach. The marsh mosquitoed
with light. Rapture, but also brevity,
in the amber glow.

Meanwhile, lovers hazarding naked
what they should have in bed.
In a dead-end bluffed with cottages
and swaying grass. A rueful gull
glancing on from the clouds.

And between love and death, what?
The cliff, a stone's throw from their preening.
Shale, brine, instability.

Tidewater maelstroming in the fingers,
throat, eardrums.

Mortality, insisting.

Or maybe just the florid spray
of surf and ledge.

Heliotrope.

Mont Royal

1

She first spied him at the epicentre,
the sun, in shambles, pivoting
breathlessly around him.

Genius? Philosopher?

Mountains, he'd said, gravitated to him
in dreams. Sermonizing, as always,
in puffed-up tongues.

Je ne rêve pas en mots, je rêve dans l'abstrait.

Which she interpreted, of course,
misinterpreted, as *strength*.

Bring on the wine.

Thus spake the Poet, his beauty scintillant.
Dawn liquifying to ambrosia.

Nervous?

No.

Lie down, then. Let me open you.

Promise you won't disappear on me.

                              Promise.

His talk dizzied her mind,
shocked its inert shapes,
bent them, at will, into lakes
and fields, the summer cosmos

reached deeper still
into the music

of her womb, vibrating
the darkest chords
into a rich, saxophone,
full-bodied cry.

In the morning dew,
mute, faint of heart,

the reticent sun started up

a pale, knock-kneed light
toeing the perimeter.

2

his loin was too fired up, because
full sun, hotter than Africa

because orgasms
like *Trudeaumania* on placards

because her hand kept turning up
in all the wrong places, between

vestiges of gobbledygook
in the Upper Crust, 1950s
arborite living

because crowds, crowds, & crowds
in migraine clusters on the soft knoll

because the air beating
tom-toms & tie-dye guitars

because juice in the Fender electric organ

& every cardinal point, engaged,
attacking

3

I'll tell you what the city was like before the earth cracked
under her feet. Before Bacchus and the bergamot
groundswell of autumn: consummate rooms
of stern commodes and catholic lace.
Ossified sets of sterling.
Housewives in their boudoirs courting impropriety.
Always of two minds in their madness.

The secrets of their fallen tresses
too big, too wrong for the solid light.

Don't blame them, blame the times: women cufflinked
to their men, dutiful.

Coffee served with petits fours. From a bird's eye,
the Paternal tea wagon holding court:

    Gloria Patri, et Filio, et Spiritui Sancto

    mea culpa, mea culpa, mea maxima culpa.

That, and a whole litany of breadcrumbs.

4

Now, let me describe the conjugated landscape:
the invisible, violet pull downward,

the nuanced air, night-zones
in a spring sweat, jittery
with neon.

As you fathom the scene, note the sultry
planet gliding out of orbit, subtle shifts into the future
perfect, a gaping open-endedness:
V radiant, the rats ravenous in her floorboards.

Note where she will have gone once she steps out
of the camisole. Her sugars pawed by the breeze.

How she will have flowered
once she severs her ties

in a brutal parting of the ways
                — her light, at last, escaping.

5

A prevailing wisdom existed — yes.
That God placed good and bad in the human brain.

And on equal footing.

Meaning an upright soul could go blind masturbating
or feeding her eyes to the flame.

She took the high road to avoid him.

Outwitting Time and the heavy artillery
of rain. Until gravity surrendered, and the good
clean earth boomeranged off course.

He caught up and sandaled ahead.

A little like Jesus on his walkabout
mesmerizing the hordes. The ecstatic,

kicked-up sand in his wake,
pinwheeling sunward.

Foolhardy, she stared into the wick,
point-blank, though she knew

she should not.

6

the Poem is her education:

a room of hardwood floors
& rain-soaked talk
        the unbroken line
of poets at the bar,
consumed

by candlelight, a sultry glass
of wine, a saxophone
in this lonely town
where the rivers meet,

a velvet matchbook
word: *Auberge*

more alluring than
Belgium, Luxembourg,
every nation

of every Byron ever put together

what the hungry
imagination pens

the overwhelming constellations
of the heart, this lingering
scent on her flesh
all these hours later

their ordinary bed
in extraordinary time

her education is   the poem
is — her life

simultaneously microscopic &
macroscopic, the spark of two
rubbed sticks & the universal éclat

7

She shadowed him like Rimbaud stalked Verlaine
(a question of scent, she *had to*), plunging

with him into the absinthe depths
until they washed up, cleansed,
in the swill of a lake.

The rest, of course, resonant
of *The Fall*: the knocked-up world,
the blood beating wrong

her mind, fouled, forsaking her,
while she took him

for Christ, bathing his feet
in her derelict breasts,

whispering unto him

the corrupt threnody
of stars

8

The beginning of the end, that old cliché, started
with flashing danger signs:

churches on the chopping block,
sex shops christening the metropolis.
Then Leary who quite literally
stole from Socrates.

Enter here, Venus, caught in the guillotine of change:
Cup to her mouth, culture on the rocks,
she "quite happily drank the poison,"
purple on the tongue, and accusatory.

The earth churned, new catechisms bubbling
to the fold. Basil the Great, black-robed,
bohemian, bearing messages.

A devious, dark cloud overhead:

The bread in your cupboard
Belongs to the hungry man.

Pimping for Heathcliff, or Morrison, or
the brooding, larger-than-life one who emptied into her,
his jumping jugular in her twistfallen hair.

9

Art caught up with her, the blurring of life and form.
Everyone from Dali to Warhol pegging his demons
on her, the scribbled cosmos.

Even the heavens made their case. Viewing her sprint
to the Abbey as strength, not weakness.

Truth, she was ducking the perilous air, searching
for walls: the monastic trees. Structure and
the monochromatic sky.

Pray, eat, sleep, pray.

Who else but God knew the threat of leaves
on her cloistered flesh? Humid, the primal

woods forced their palette and range.
Vigils. Compline. Terce. Offerings

of what he could do to her. If only.
The creek, at her thighs, widened.

Again and again, she violated herself
in the savage moss,
then at Vespers under the sculpted dome.

Her rouged mind conjuring the divine
sloth of Jesus on the cross.

What, in Christ's name, would he do
if she let him? The Brothers knew.

Her lithe neck
had barely escaped him, alive.

10

Contrary to popular lore, he was no cartoon,
no roadside snake, no Jekyl-and-Hyde
genital-hacking wolf in sheep's clothes.

Not an ounce of gun-loving yawp in his hands.

But an enigma, all the same. Sharpshooter firing
from the hip. The Charlie Manson of Letters,
opening her surreptitiously from the top down.

Pollinating her tongue with a lick
of verse, a glass of something-or-other.

The moon, at a safe haul, ratifying the talk.
Baying frequently and in technicolour.

Metaphorically, *of course.*

11

It is one thing to imagine, another to act.
Murder would not have been out of the question.
Poisoning the food supply. Anything, anything
for a racy touch. Their bluespot in the flame
away from the rational metropolis.

Peace, order & good government.

His wife.

His wife in her silk kimono, bulked up on sanity.
Conjuring the Sages out of thin air:

The cleverest doctor cannot save himself.

Nothing turned up.

No secluded café, no rat-squeeze
off the beaten highway, nothing.

She bookmarked her page, then called it a night.
Man has a thousand schemes; Heaven, one.

Letters (1)

1

Teacher —
Rescue me from academe
& ride me as Leonard
did Suzanne. *Away.*

Fly me to the fulcrum
of the candyfloss fair.
Up & up, again.

In your *beautiful balloon.*

2

Lorraine Motel, April 4th:
Memphis dystopia. Junior
Martin Luther King
frenching the Grim Reaper.

Crows darkening Baltimore, Boston, Chicago,
Detroit, Kansas City, Newark, Washington —

46 deaths, all told.

And on the June train to Arlington,
gene-dust dressed for the cemetery:

another Kennedy.

Tell me, how can I be your student of Love
while light rains down around us

one bullet at a time?

3

By what right do I commune with the hooded monks,
my own modest chapel stained in blood?

What divine light do I gather here
in full menstrual éclat?

Sweetened in my underthings. Undeserving.

Hours snake through the chaste dome
while I shed my skin, shameless in my slither

down from God to Man.

To the amphibian Sacrament. Where monster-headed

and in declension, I drink of the chalice
that pours abundance into the arched gateway

of my throat. Hymn flooding through me,
marrying the wet knot of heaven

between my thighs.

4

To desire is not to name every river, not to separate
the swooning birds or the ample-thighed magnolias
from their sky. But to let spring bloat

into every stalled memory: me rough-housed
against a car, a little of the blue-and-white
narcissus within. A little Diana.

Remember how I hunted your mouth
in the dark, begging for more?

"It isn't enough," I said.
And your sane reply: "My wife."

You offered some one-last-time
hard, before kick-starting down the road.
Victorian, almost, in your resistance.

Add some years, and I'll remember it differently:
humidity leaking from the fairy-tale clouds

weather in all the wrong places, agitation,

more adulation than *politesse.*
Greed. The carmine swale devouring.

Let me paint you a picture —

Eve in the arboretum mounting a tree,
her moist constellation
suckered to the colossus.

His snaking hands from behind, from the rooted
clay earth, discovering her.

Venus

1

It's not that we didn't learn right from wrong in school.
We just never bought it.

Don't think of our hands, prim on the page,
making icons

of the alphabet. Think how our knees sat tight
under catholic kilts, secretive. Waiting

for the lapsed darkness, a tiny crack in the wall
of nuns shadowing our every thought.

Think of us stealing light, scarfing it down, famished.
Our broken commandment
we would pay for, later, in spades

because what we truly craved was perennial
afternoon, the playground beyond the cinderblock:
dandelions sunning their bellies, dahlias
in taffeta blushing from the sidelines.

What we desired, unequivocally, was lush
labial fruit. Our very own wet spot
flowering within. Not Holy Floods

and Paradise, but the whole endorphin world
gushing from our pores.

2

The revolution lasted 365 days.

Beatles spooling into psychedelic summer,
the peppermint sky ringed in light.

Your fingers fed me
oranges from a Dutch-blue plate
while his "just society"
tingled in our midst.

You, too, were charismatic. Stringing me along
a new and dangerous arc.

Imagine, not even cringing when I heard those words
from my own mouth,

the fearless, poppied spin of them —

Hurt me. So I come back to you.

3

Never am I not pondering an alternate reality.
Whether on foot through the spruce woods
or within the cool sherbet of ocean tints.

Toddler pokes about, scavenging for "gold"
      — clams, seaglass, quartz

but even the starry awe he wears
like an oversized shirt is nothing

next to the sandpiper
penciling its simple path
through mauve and imagined dawn.

Because the mind is bigger and more powerful.

A wolf pine paws up in every direction,
and all roads point inward to memory and
the tangled spread of consciousness.

What I mean to write, I won't for fear:
"She" in hot pursuit of our paper trail.
Darkness bleeding through the clouds.

Even here, in the filtered sunlight
beneath trees,
I speak only in whispers.

4

Butterfly in apricot dusk, stilled
long enough to picture it

otherwise: leaf

of exquisite notepaper, or
the finest, pleated Japanese silk.

Whose printed wing,
lampshade gold,
could be the telltale
of every sumptuous secret, or
the diminutive, postcard universe.

Its muted markings nibbed in ink:
Wish you were here.

Code for all I would say.

5

I was air before words ignited
in my mouth: *take me, wreck me*

the incendiary blaze

branding me to you, intensifying
our communal noise.

      Larger than life, we explode in stars.

No shared history,
no glue to stop the universe
from self-destructing.

Only madness & our own invigorating
run from death.

Cramming time we don't have with audacity,
with napalm & our quaking
upstart cells.

Until we fall away from the pyre,
centred & feverish,

      dangerously alive.

As for the places we've been & left:
see how quickly ash fills in.

A bungalow in the suburbs,
repetitive walls of grey on grey.
People soft-shoeing about, loath
to upset the furniture.

And on the Mountain, a cold empty space
above the trampled weed

where we never walked.

Mont Royal

1

He joins her, mid-phrase,
putting a stop. Plugging up holes
as they occur: potentiality. He's had it
with smoking guns, combustible
noun-verb combinations.

Crackling exposition.

Both of them standing there:
matchsticks by an oil slick.
Her palate pressurized
into its usual firetrap.
Touch me —
I want —

No, he piffles
dousing the flame.
His conjugal riposte.

Cool.
Just *no*.

2

What's kept her afloat all these weeks?
What drags her from one dun moment
to the next? The abyss

of minutiae: the April sheen of his skin,
sundaying over breakfast, the vertigo light
refracted in their talk. An argument,

however, builds for the oncoming cars,
a calculated step into their brutal headlights,
her silhouette, filmy, dissolving

in the mist. The spill of grief not as wreckage —
explosive, expansive — but as raindrops
butterflying off the highway.

3

There were places, galore, for disgrace.
Drab, sepia spaces

the colour of tongues in absentia
drifting in wait. Dickensian

realms where girls holding hands
with the devil

went for a chilly dose of Mother Superior.
Others rolled the dice, instead.

Gambling on a state of grace,
a stay of execution:

the warmed basement flat,
the bathtub, the sacred
wire hanger.

Singing, somehow, with a strength of angels
when they should have been burning.

4

Call her what you will. Coy but irrepressible Eve
opened her Garden of worms so God could create
his acerbic tableau: old-hat couple stewing
over Paradise. Painted into a corner
of terrazzo and vine.

Picture Flemish darkness, the subjects
fashionably moribund.

Imagine all the wrong colours,
a last spittering candle between them.

Watch how the forms themselves etherize
on contact. How they vanish into the umber,
knowing that one small cough
won't change the course of events.

He could well have painted them into the
sheep-dotted hills of England. Properly
bland and very, very British.

A pair of porcelain cups, mindful of their own
mutual fragility.
Certain that life is about one thing
and one thing only:

containing the spillage.

If only they could muster a boisterous heart,
some bugled adrenaline.

The palpitating pigments of Titian on a fertile day.

5

Summer hums with improvised gaiety.
In a parallel hemisphere.

Birdsong in ascending scale. Dawn gladdened
with mangrove, eucalyptus. Jubilant

over-the-moon kids promising
all the wrong things to each other.

So rapt, so absorbed in their own rhythm,
they're unaware of the storm

making overtures on the horizon.

Because living hasn't yet tapered off into
Satie's sad piano.

Yes, the rest of the world seems to know

a thing or two about love's bitter edge,
the dirge that wells up, unannounced,

to drown the Orphean blue. But who will say?
Having been there themselves. Having known

what it means to drag among the baritones,
but before that, what it really is to fly.

Letters (II)

1

You showed me how to love you
in a dark hotel

spring's thin hymen
torn in two.

And in the *Joon Café*
below our bed
a fortune cookie spoke
our "crime": prudence
out the window,

shredded.

You've ruined me
and I am jealous now
of everything —
the air that breathed you first,

water, wind, and rain,

what covets you at dawn
while I'm asleep:

the amorous, cornflower light.

2

How that "her" triggers in me
the unseemly.

Whitest of doberman teeth, blood
in my damien hackles.

How I flourish, now, in the howling
rogue jazz of my mind

animalvegetablemineral

while my body absconds with
the moderate world, sleepwalking
among stick figures &
the ho-hum trees.

3

Baby drives a wedge.
Casts our days in a bluish pall.

Where once we lived, thrived,
pleasurably.

I tell you, I'd open a vein.

Freefall into hell's
gnashing turbines.

But you —

with your curt words
& cold coffee

— you are stone now.

Objectifying the world.
Analyzing things
as mere things

in your life:
Credit cards,
your sometimes-wife.

This water glass on my table
half full, half
empty.

4

As though a pilgrimage to the mournful
blooms would lessen your transgression.

A solitary pose by the Judas tree
in the judicial light of day.

Your flagrant, look-see sores
interminably seeking their salve.

As though the righteous, teacup world
would pardon you

if you laboured long enough,
hard enough. If you suffered

(played) exquisitely.

*Me voici dans les dégats de la lumière
et ton âme, cette noirceur,*

*mon amour, cette lourdeur
parfois amère.*

5

After three days, one eats again;
After three months, one washes again;
After a year, one wears raw silk again
under the garment of mourning.

— Such abundance from Confucius.

Still, I would drink the wine
one last time

from your lips.

6

Brown, the bedridden talk
of applecores & candywrap.
Commiserating:

*When death has already paled
our cheeks, other roses
will be flowering.*

Parkbench wino, say,
huddled under newsprint.
Dispossessed.

I wonder:

Was that our love-child I saw today
matted in the laneway?

The insects investigating her
for crumbs. Best conjure

her there in the anonymous
junk of pipes

than admit she's gone

missing. Not flogged to death, not
raped, but poured, unforgivably,

through a fault in the earth.

Rose

1

We are thrust into places.

Me, in my gated community, flawed;
you, stitching your way through the glaucous rain.

Hard to know who came first, the chicken
or the egg. Gossamer, nymph

of spun gold, I was there, incognito,
in an alcove of your brain,

a tentative, woolly confection attaching itself
to your dreams, though I, too, dreamt —
primordial dreams.

You, solid steel, butting through the eye of spring,
not thread, but silver lining, formidable.

Pure Idea, you were this:
cloudburst locomotive forging ahead

and in your wake, fortified,
the woven land.

2

You cave and he takes you
into hiding, a rat's throw
from Leo's Laundromat
and the 24/7 Exterminator.

(Where the bedraggled gather,
fishbowl bellies dragging
in the subaqueous light.)

Where, together, you dangle me
over the precipice —

bloodmeal for Poseidon

— before reeling me back,
slickened, unharmed.

Your minds on the walk home
sanitizing the scene,

mollifying your sin with a rose
and a word

for what is undulating,
uncharted, in trust.

3

The city awoke, refurbished. Yesterday's euphony
of rain easing into birdsong.

After the long night, quiet restoration.

But whatever happened to those lovers
singing the raspberry blush of dawn?

I ask not out of anger or spite,
but out of genuine sorrow.

Sometimes, second thoughts
bear no resemblance
to second thoughts:

their failure to accommodate
the fluctuating light.

A rosebush beneath the window.
The last warbling stars,

bending away.

4

"Nulle Part" is nowhere
dans la langue de Molière,
concrete club in the fug of town
where kooks kick ass, or kick
the proverbial bucket
in a piss-drunk show

for brooms on the sidelines:
losers on barstools, linted with years
of the same-old same.
You know the type.

Clouding the room with their dusty
marriages and sweeping tales of woe.
Old-school bleeding hearts
wearing shock with neutrality:
a bristled, sideways glance.

Flatlined. Regardless of this or that
scuffle on the floor,

ducat scudding through a jukebox,
jingling the nether with a can-can,
a curtsy, and a goodbye pair
of dancing shoes.

5

To the Romantics,
I dance out in style,

Seagrams in hand, quarters
capsizing the jukebox.

Body shrunken to a tail, eeling,
rudderless, into the murk.

Incommunicado.

Tongue and vertebrae slushed to silt.

The shell of my former self
toe-tapping its Broadway finale,
its curtain call,

its not-so-Hollywood ending.

The tired night awash
in the flotsam-and-jetsam,

relinquishing its residual grip.

Clotted, now, in rivulets
on the floor.

6

Like mint unhinging itself
in the wind, a dwindled

green-eyed scent.

Or summer in a squirrel's mouth,
startled away. I surrendered.

When Eden detonated, I bunkered
AWOL in the moon's hushed phase

holing, head-first, underground,
out of bounds. Resurfacing

in the whispered innuendo
of ordinary things misplaced
or fallen between the cracks,

lipsticks, brooches

their lacklustre prints still
soldiering among the shadows.

7

Here's the nerves-of-steel epitaph
I'd have liked: *Martyr for the Cause,*

dead before the Last Spike

immortalized for her sharded remains
in the jaws of a tree, unrelenting:
a partial foot

origins unknown, the driven
Jane Doe
dragging tubs of nitroglycerin
across the stubborn Shield

yielding, with splendor,
to an errant rock,

ribcage smithereened

while the newborn land held on

and on.

8

Because I've come this far
I can say what I want to say.

Because the lights are dim & wanting.

Because I've looked squarely into the face of the devil.
Because I gambled with the Fates & lost.

Because the racing clock has lulled
long enough for me to state my peace.

Don't look surprised.

Everyone's heard of the death-row damned
in his last poignant hour. Fumbling in the dark
with his erroneous heart,
the wrong set of keys.

Because I'm here now
at the kitchen table
across from the empty chair
where she sits in her pale robe,

invisible.

Because of that groggy inmate
on the serum road to sleep.
Praying for a lifeline,
an out-of-the-blue miracle.

Because we all know that none of it will come:
the cinematic knock at the door
quickening the pulse,

the desperate, last-ditch phone call,
the voice on the other end,
chipper, wired for spring,
saying *hello*.

Requiem

Love that does not destroy is not real love.
— Omar Khayyam

Notes

Venus smiles not in a house of tears – from William Shakespeare, *Romeo and Juliet*, Act IV, sc. I

Three Wise Men — a reference to Trudeau as one of the three politicians who went to Ottawa in the 1960s to fight for "French Power." The others were Jean Marchand and Gérard Pelletier. This poem refers to Trudeau's famous "walk in the snow" on February 28, 1984 when he decided to resign for the second and final time, stating: I walked until midnight in the storm...I listened to my heart and saw if there were any signs of my destiny in the sky, and there were none — there were just snowflakes.

hemlines on the rise, the city walls, shaking — adapted from Timothy Leary's *Jail Notes*, Grove Press, Inc.: New York, 1970. As quoted from Plato: "When the mode of the music changes, the walls of the city shake." (8)

Micha — nickname of Pierre and Margaret Trudeau's youngest son, Michel, 23, who died tragically in an avalanche in British Columbia on November 13, 1998.

We desired a god, bedrock, the model / Spartan, mind and muscle / armed for calamity / insurrection — These lines inspired from Gordon Donaldson's book *The Prime Ministers of Canada*, Doubleday of Canada Ltd., 1994. (239-241)

Maudit traître — goddam traitor

Zeno of Elea — Greek philosopher (c.490-c.430 B.C.) who devised a number of arguments to prove the unreality of motion, the most famous being the paradox of Achilles and the tortoise.

He who does not imagine a stronger and better light / Than his perishing and mortal eye can see, / Does not imagine at all — from William Blake, "The Prophets."

Je ne rêve pas en mots, je rêve dans l'abstrait — I don't dream in words, I dream in abstractions. (The character here has actually lifted these words from something Pierre Trudeau once said to Margaret early in their relationship.)

Gloria Patri, et Filio, et Spiritui Sancto / mea culpa, mea culpa, mea maxima culpa — from *Le Catechisme des Provinces Ecclesiastiques de Quebec*, Montreal et Ottawa, Edition Officielle, 1944.

she quite happily drank the poison — adapted from Timothy Leary, *Jail Notes*. (96)

The bread in your cupboard / Belongs to the hungry man — as quoted from Basil the Great, 365 A.D.

Me voici dans les dégats de la lumière / et ton âme, cette noirceur, / mon amour, cette lourdeur/ parfois amère — I am caught in the spoils of the light and your soul. The darkness, my Love, the weight of it, occasionally bitter.

When death has already paled our cheeks, / other roses / will be flowering — from Omar Khayyam's *Ruba'iyat*.

Penultimate poem — liberally adapted from Mary Fitzgibbon, *A Trip to Manitoba: Or Roughing It on the Line*, Rose-Belford Publishing, Toronto, 1880. (163)

All references to the "train" or the building of a railway refer to the building of the Canadian Pacific Railway, John A. Macdonald's dream project intended to join the country, solidify the "union."